Success in Spelling

Level 4

By

Rebecca McSpadden Avery

ISBN 1-58095-864-8

The Weaver Curriculum Company
PO Box 7438
Chandler, AZ 85246-7438
(888) 367-9871

Notice of Copyright

Dear Friend,

I am pleased to introduce to you *Success in Spelling*, a program designed to help children obtain successful spelling techniques. It has been said that good spellers are born. This is not true. It is true that spelling comes easier for some than for others, and there is evidence that the primary function of the brain effects that process. However, good spellers are those who not only can memorize and remember how a word LOOKS, but also the rules which apply to spelling.

Phonics (the decoding of words) and spelling go hand in hand, especially in the early levels of spelling. As the child progresses, spelling rules take over where phonic rules end. *Success in Spelling* integrates phonic rules and spelling rules at the proper time.

Spelling should not be taught until the child is reading fluently. It should not be taught in conjunction with reading, but after the child can read. Language has a natural order of progression. It flows from hearing the word said, to reading, to spelling (or writing). *Success in Spelling* **follows that progression.**

Success in Spelling has been created because I had an overwhelming need in my own home–school for a successful spelling program. After trying traditional approaches, I began to research styles of teaching spelling. The pretest/formula style has been very successful in schools, and has proven even more successful in the home school. Giving the child word lists from which to begin, the child then sifts through the list to determine the known from the unknown. The words not known are then emphasized. When daily creative writing is applied to the process of spelling, success is obtained. Since writing (composition) is an entire subject on its own, we suggest *Success in Spelling* be used in conjunction with *Wisdom Words*, a complete Grammar and Composition program available through *The Weaver Curriculum*.

I would like to welcome you to this program. It makes the task of teaching spelling easy!

Towards Success in Spelling,
Becky Avery

Introduction

Success in Spelling is a program designed for spelling success. Emphasis within this program is placed in three areas: phonic rules as they apply to spelling, proper study habits which will lead to good spelling, and a method of review for reinforcement purposes. Spelling is only beneficial when the child can apply it to writing. Spelling has its only purpose in writing. Therefore, writing must accompany any spelling program. It is the suggestion of the author that *Wisdom Words*, a complete Grammar and Composition program available through *The Weaver* be used to further implement the words learned in the spelling lessons. Directions for writing are included within *Wisdom Words*.

Level 4 contains two kinds of word listings:
1. **A Master Spelling List** for the teacher. The Master Spelling List gives you all of the spelling words by lesson number and includes diacritical markings and syllabication for each word.
2. **Pretest Lesson Forms** for the student with the words printed on them. The level and the number of the lesson are at the bottom right corner of each pretest sheet.

There are weekly instructions containing day–by–day assignments and activities to implement the program. Assignments include writing the words, finding the meaning of the words, doing diacritical markings and syllabication. Activities include games and memory reinforcement. The formula for good spelling is also broken down into a daily routine.

When you are ready to give the student the pretest, remove the page from the book. Fold the test on the first dotted line, folding the word list to the back. Hand the pretest to the child with the middle column facing up, so that all the child sees is the blank spaces. Find the correct number on your Master Spelling List and call out the words for the child to spell, one at a time. The child writes the word as he thinks it is spelled. After all the words have been given, the child unfolds the paper and compares the correct spelling (already typed words) with the way he spelled the word. Words that are not spelled correctly are written in the third column. Train the child to emphasize the part of the word misspelled by CAPITALIZING that section of the word. For example, if the child misspelled the word *came* as *cam*, he would write it in the third column as *camE*.

It is important to remember that the pretest is NOT a final test, but rather a test to see what the child already knows. There is no sense in teaching what the child already knows. A final test is given on the fifth day of the week (instructions are in the daily instruction section of each lesson). Should the child still misspell words, these words then become next week's spelling words. A blank pretest form has been provided at the back of the book for his purpose. The blank pretest may be copied. Copy several at one time and save for the times they are needed.

As you continue with the pretest format, look carefully at the words your child has difficulty spelling. Is there a pattern to the words he misses? If so, it is an indication of a phonic rule or spelling rule he doesn't know. Teach that rule to him (again and again if necessary).

Level 4 is not indicative of any particular grade level. It is, instead, indicative of a progression in spelling. It is the author's suggestion that this spelling level be started only with children in fifth grade and above who have completed Levels 1–3 of *Success in Spelling*, and who are reading fluently. In other words, you don't teach the child to spell what he cannot read. Reading comes first, spelling second.

Begin teaching with the first lesson of this level, even if you are sure that the child knows these words. Review is a natural part of teaching, and the few minutes that it takes to review these words will benefit the student greatly. Continue to go through the lessons at a rapid pace until the student has reached the correct level. You will know the student is at the correct level when, in the pretest, he begins to miss 30–50 percent of the words on the list. If the first few lessons within this level seem too hard for the student, return to level 3 and begin to teach from that level. Information on diacritical marking and syllabication may be found on Pages 6–8.

In addition to the 66 level 4 lessons, there are 17 pretest forms containing Quickie Words which are labels as Level: Grade 5. Quickie Words are words which do not necessarily follow phonetic patterns. They are also words which are most commonly used. After you have finished the lessons, use the pretests to determine which of the Quickie Words the child needs to memorize. Be sure these are memorized before continuing on to the following level.

If you have followed the formula for spelling as detailed in the daily instructions, and have completed several lists wherein the child has correctly spelled the word, and then find the child cannot spell the word when writing, have the child look up toward the ceiling to the left, keeping his head in a straight–forward position. If he still cannot spell the word, the child should be checked for learning difficulties, and a tactile approach should be used in learning, combined with therapy. *Success in Spelling* may be used for remedial work. To do so, simply use the pretest forms as directed above, but taking longer to go through the words, until you reach the point wherein the student is accurately spelling 80 percent of the words.

There are five levels within *Success in Spelling*. All levels should be completed no later than grade six. The pace at which you progress will be determined by the student's progress. When the student has completed Level 4, progress to Level 5.

Diacritical Marks

Diacritical marks are the marks placed on words to indicate how the vowels are pronounced and the syllable emphasis. We have listed the major diacritical markings for you. Other diacritical markings may be taught when teaching a foreign language. Teach and apply them in numerical order.

1. **ó**   acute accent – used to accent the syllable to be given more emphasis. Example: wón–der–ful

2. **ŏ**   breve – used to mark a short vowel. Example: hŏt

3. **ā**   macron – used to mark a long vowel sound. Example: tā–ble

4. **ç**   cedilla – used under a *c* to show that it should be pronounced like *s*. Used only when *c* comes before an *a*, *o*, or *u* in certain words. Example: fa–çade

5. **ñ**   tilde – placed over n in Spanish words to denote addition of y to the word. Example: cañon (pronounced as can–yon), or señor (pronounced as sen–yor)

6. **ä**   schwa or dieresis – used with vowels to indicate an alternative pronunciation or to show that the second vowel is to be pronounced in a separate syllable. Example: fäther and fär or näive and Noël.

7. **à**   grave accent – used to indicate a secondary accent on a syllable. Differs from acute accent in that it is usually a lighter accent. It can also be used to show that a word is pronounced with one more syllable than usual. Example: àdvertìsement and belovèd. Also used in foreign words.

Other Possible Markings:

à	as in	fàst, glàss, a-làs´; also as in so'dà, a-dapt'à-ble.
ạ	as in	fạll, pạw, ạw'ful, ap-plạud´.
o͡o	as in	mo͡on, co͡o, fo͡od, bro͡od'er.
ö	as in	möve, pröve, tömb.
ụ	as in	bụll, pụt, fụl-fil´, boun'ti-fụl.
u̇	as in	bru̇te, ju̇'ry.
ã	as in	cãre, ãir, mil'i-tãr-y, de-clãre´.
ẽ	as in	hẽr, vẽrse, sẽr'vice, in-tẽr´.
c̲	as in	c̲at, to-bac̲'c̲o.
ṣ	as in	mi'ṣer, aṣ.
ọ	as in	lọng, crọss, ọff, ọrb, fọr-bid´, dọr'mer.

NOTE: Diacritical markings are difficult because it is hard to establish the degree of accuracy desired. Emphasis of syllables and basic vowel sounds is adequate for grammar school.

Syllabication

Knowing when to divide syllables is of extreme importance when teaching vocabulary. Syllabication should be introduced in phonics, taught in reading and reinforced in spelling. For the older child encountering long words, syllabication rules are very helpful. They give the student the power to decipher any word. At the foundation of syllabication is a very simple rule which states that every syllable must have only one vowel sound. In addition to this, other rules are added for divided syllable. Teach the rules listed below in the order given. Be certain to provide adequate opportunity for application.

1.   A consonant between two vowels tends to go with the second vowel unless the first vowel is accented and short. Example: bro–ken, wag–on

2.   Divide two consonants between vowels unless they are a blend or digraph. Example: pic–ture, ush–er

3.   When there are three consonants between two vowels, divide between the blend or the digraph and the other consonant. Example: an–gler

4.   Prefixes always form separate syllables, and suffixes form separate syllables only in the following cases:

    a.   The suffix tends to pick up the preceding consonant. Example: fligh–ty

    b.   The suffix –*ed* tends to form a separate syllable only when it follows a root that ends in *d* or *t'*. Example: plant–ed

    c.   The suffix –*s* never forms a syllable except when it follows an *e*. Example: at–oms, cours–es

5.   Always divide compound words. Example: black–bird

6.   Final *le* picks up the preceding consonant to form a syllable. Example: ta–ble

7. Do not split common vowel clusters, such as:

   a. R–controlled vowels (ar, er, ir, and ur). Example: ar–ti–cle

   b. Long vowel digraphs (ea, ee, ai, oa, and ow). Example: fea–ture

   c. Broad *o* clusters (au, aw, and al). Example: au–di–ence

   d. Diphthongs (oi, oy, and ow). Example: thou–sand

   e. Double *o* like *oo*. Example: moon

8. Vowel Problems: Every syllable must have one and only one vowel sound.

   a. The letter *e* at the end of a word is silent. Example: come

   b. The letter *y* at the end or in the middle of a word operates as a vowel. Example: ver–y, cy–cle

   c. Two vowels together with separate sounds form separate syllables. Example: po–li–o

Level 4, Numbers 1–2

Day 1

Introduce the spelling words. Have the child say each word.

Hand the child the pretest sheet so that he can see this week's spelling words.

This lesson deals with homophones, words that sound alike or similar, but are spelled differently and have different meanings. The spelling and the meaning is important. When introducing these words, explain to your child the meaning of the word. Use the words in a sentence in context.

Day 2

Activity: Play *Chinese English*. To play, write the first letter of each word very large. Then write each of the other letters within the word tucked around the large letter. Be creative.

Day 3

Give the child the pretest. Find the correct word list in your master spelling list and call out the words for the child to spell, one at a time. If the child can spell every word correctly, discontinue this lesson (the child is successful) and go on to the next lesson. If the child misses any word or combination of words, continue on with the following instructions.

Day 4

The child's missed words on the pretest are now the words that the child needs to study. Teach your child to have good study habits. Use this formula:

(1) Look at the word. Say it.
(2) Close your eyes and spell the word. Check to see if you are correct. If not, start over.
(3) Cover the word and write it. Check to see if you are correct. If not, start over.
(4) Repeat this procedure three times for each word missed on the pretest.

Day 5

Repeat the study process for each word. Taking the child's pretest list, give the child a final written test on the words missed on the pretest. When taking the final test, require the child to write the word in a sentence. Words missed on the final test are automatically added to the next lesson.

Level 4, Numbers 3–4

Day 1

Introduce the spelling words. Have the child say each word.

Hand the child the pretest sheet so that he can see this week's spelling words. Ask the child to explain the meaning of each word.

This lesson contains words which are accented on the last syllable. Divide each word into syllables, placing the accent on the last syllable. Your Master Spelling List gives you the correct syllabication for each word. Use the words in a sentence in context.

Day 2

Activity: Giving your child a copy of the pretest, have the child write each word divided into syllables, with the accent on the last syllable, and each vowel marked with the proper diacritical mark. Have the child write a short story using 12 of the words within this lesson.

Day 3

Give the child the pretest. Find the correct word list in your master spelling list and call out the words for the child to spell, one at a time. If the child can spell every word correctly, discontinue this lesson (the child is successful) and go on to the next lesson. If the child misses any word or combination of words, continue on with the following instructions.

Day 4

The child's missed words on the pretest are now the words that the child needs to study. Teach your child to have good study habits. Use this formula:

    (1) Look at the word. Say it.
    (2) Close your eyes and spell the word. Check to see if you are correct. If not, start over.
    (3) Cover the word and write it. Check to see if you are correct. If not, start over.
    (4) Repeat this procedure three times for each word missed on the pretest.

Day 5

Repeat the study process for each word. Taking the child's pretest list, give the child a final written test on the words missed on the pretest. When taking the final test, require the child to write the word in a sentence. Words missed on the final test are automatically added to the next lesson.

Day 1

Introduce the spelling words. Have the child say each word.

Hand the child the pretest sheet so that he can see this week's spelling words. Ask the child to explain the meaning of each word.

The words within this lesson are accented on the first syllable. Introduce the words by dividing the words into syllables, placing the accent on the first syllable. Your Master Spelling List gives you the correct syllabication for each word. Use the words in a sentence in context.

Day 2

Activity: Giving your child a list of the words, have the child divide each word into syllables, accenting the first syllable, and marking each vowel with the proper diacritical mark. Play the game *The Minister's Cat*. To play, the teacher begins with the sentence *"The minister's cat is an alley cat."* The child then says *"The minister's cat is an alley cat who came in **contact** with a deacon's cat."* The word **contact** is one of this week's spelling words. Now it is the teacher's turn: *"The minister's cat is an alley cat who came in contact with a deacon's cat. The deacon's cat had three eyes and one **nostril**."* The child continues the game by repeating everything that was said so far, adding another sentence in which one of the spelling words is used. The game ends at your discretion.

Day 3

Give the child the pretest. Find the correct word list in your master spelling list and call out the words for the child to spell, one at a time. If the child can spell every word correctly, discontinue this lesson (the child is successful) and go on to the next lesson. If the child misses any word or combination of words, continue on with the following instructions.

Day 4

The child's missed words on the pretest are now the words that the child needs to study. Teach your child to have good study habits. Use this formula:

(1) Look at the word. Say it.
(2) Close your eyes and spell the word. Check to see if you are correct. If not, start over.
(3) Cover the word and write it. Check to see if you are correct. If not, start over.
(4) Repeat this procedure three times for each word missed on the pretest.

Day 5

Repeat the study process for each word. Taking the child's pretest list, give the child a final written test on the words missed on the pretest. When taking the final test, require the child to write the word in a sentence. Words missed on the final test are automatically added to the next lesson.

Level 4, Numbers 7–8

Day 1

Introduce the spelling words. Have the child say each word.

Hand the child the pretest sheet so that he can see this week's spelling words. Ask the child to explain the meaning of each word.

This lesson teaches monosyllables. Introduce the words by marking each vowel with the proper diacritical mark. Diacritical markings and syllabication are all done for you in the Master Spelling List. Use the words in a sentence in context.

Day 2

Activity: After the child has marked the diacritical marking on each vowel of each word, play the game *I Am Thinking*. Begin by saying *"I am thinking of a spelling word. It rhymes with smeared."* The word is **beard**. It is then the child's turn. You may use any clues you wish, describing spelling of the word, such as *"This word has two ee's at the end."*

Day 3

Give the child the pretest. Find the correct word list in your master spelling list and call out the words for the child to spell, one at a time. If the child can spell every word correctly, discontinue this lesson (the child is successful) and go on to the next lesson. If the child misses any word or combination of words, continue on with the following instructions.

Day 4

The child's missed words on the pretest are now the words that the child needs to study. Teach your child to have good study habits. Use this formula:

    (1) Look at the word. Say it.
    (2) Close your eyes and spell the word. Check to see if you are correct. If not, start over.
    (3) Cover the word and write it. Check to see if you are correct. If not, start over.
    (4) Repeat this procedure three times for each word missed on the pretest.

Day 5

Repeat the study process for each word. Taking the child's pretest list, give the child a final written test on the words missed on the pretest. When taking the final test, require the child to write the word in a sentence. Words missed on the final test are automatically added to the next lesson.

Level 4, Numbers 9–10

Day 1

Introduce the spelling words. Have the child say each word.

Hand the child the pretest sheet so that he can see this week's spelling words. Ask the child to explain the meaning of each word.

The words in this lesson emphasize the accent of the second syllable. To introduce the words, divide them into syllables, placing the accent on the first syllable. Diacritical markings and syllabication are all done for you in the Master Spelling List. Use the words in a sentence in context.

Day 2

Activity: After dividing each word into syllables, placing the accent on the second syllable and marking each vowel with diacritical marks, have the child play *Buffaloon*. To play, two spelling words are combined. You may leave out duplicate spelling letters if you wish. For example, *ecstatic* and *elastic* may be added together to achieve *ecstaticelastic*.

Day 3

Give the child the pretest. Find the correct word list in your master spelling list and call out the words for the child to spell, one at a time. If the child can spell every word correctly, discontinue this lesson (the child is successful) and go on to the next lesson. If the child misses any word or combination of words, continue on with the following instructions.

Day 4

The child's missed words on the pretest are now the words that the child needs to study. Teach your child to have good study habits. Use this formula:

(1) Look at the word. Say it.
(2) Close your eyes and spell the word. Check to see if you are correct. If not, start over.
(3) Cover the word and write it. Check to see if you are correct. If not, start over.
(4) Repeat this procedure three times for each word missed on the pretest.

Day 5

Repeat the study process for each word. Taking the child's pretest list, give the child a final written test on the words missed on the pretest. When taking the final test, require the child to write the word in a sentence. Words missed on the final test are automatically added to the next lesson.

Level 4, Numbers 11–12

Day 1

Introduce the spelling words. Have the child say each word.

Hand the child the pretest sheet so that he can see this week's spelling words. Ask the child to explain the meaning of each word.

This lesson begins with words that are accented on the second syllable and continues into homophones. Require the child to divide each word into syllables and to record the meaning of each word. Your Master Spelling List gives you the correct syllabication for each word. Use the words in a sentence in context.

Day 2

Activity: Have the child give you a verbal sentence for each word.

Day 3

Give the child the pretest. Find the correct word list in your master spelling list and call out the words for the child to spell, one at a time. If the child can spell every word correctly, discontinue this lesson (the child is successful) and go on to the next lesson. If the child misses any word or combination of words, continue on with the following instructions.

Day 4

The child's missed words on the pretest are now the words that the child needs to study. Teach your child to have good study habits. Use this formula:

(1) Look at the word. Say it.
(2) Close your eyes and spell the word. Check to see if you are correct. If not, start over.
(3) Cover the word and write it. Check to see if you are correct. If not, start over.
(4) Repeat this procedure three times for each word missed on the pretest.

Day 5

Repeat the study process for each word. Taking the child's pretest list, give the child a final written test on the words missed on the pretest. When taking the final test, require the child to write the word in a sentence. Words missed on the final test are automatically added to the next lesson.

Day 1

Introduce the spelling words. Have the child say each word.

Hand the child the pretest sheet so that he can see this week's spelling words. Ask the child to explain the meaning of each word.

This lesson trains the child in words that are accented on the last syllable. To introduce the words, have the child divide each word into syllables, adding the accent on the proper syllable. Diacritical markings and syllabication are all done for you in the Master Spelling List. Use the words in a sentence in context.

Day 2

Activity: Choose one of the spelling words. Write it vertically on the board. Using other spelling words, fill in the letters. See the following for an example:

    Below
    Ensue
   re**M**ote
dep**O**rt
    Afloat
   i**N**flict

Continue until all the words have been used.

Day 3

Give the child the pretest. Find the correct word list in your master spelling list and call out the words for the child to spell, one at a time. If the child can spell every word correctly, discontinue this lesson (the child is successful) and go on to the next lesson. If the child misses any word or combination of words, continue on with the following instructions.

Day 4

The child's missed words on the pretest are now the words that the child needs to study. Teach your child to have good study habits. Use this formula:

      (1) Look at the word. Say it.
      (2) Close your eyes and spell the word. Check to see if you are correct. If not, start over.
      (3) Cover the word and write it. Check to see if you are correct. If not, start over.
      (4) Repeat this procedure three times for each word missed on the pretest.

Day 5

Repeat the study process for each word. Taking the child's pretest list, give the child a final written test on the words missed on the pretest. When taking the final test, require the child to write the word in a sentence. Words missed on the final test are automatically added to the next lesson.

Level 4, Numbers 15–16

Day 1

Introduce the spelling words. Have the child say each word.

Hand the child the pretest sheet so that he can see this week's spelling words. Ask the child to explain the meaning of each word.

This lesson reviews the long sound of vowels. Introduce the words by breaking them into syllables and marking the vowel that is long with a macron. Diacritical markings and syllabication are all done for you in the Master Spelling List. Use the words in a sentence in context.

Day 2

Activity: Play the game *Twenty Questions*. Choosing a word from the spelling list, permit the child to ask 20 questions about it, until the point where he can guess the word you have chosen.

Day 3

Give the child the pretest. Find the correct word list in your master spelling list and call out the words for the child to spell, one at a time. If the child can spell every word correctly, discontinue this lesson (the child is successful) and go on to the next lesson. If the child misses any word or combination of words, continue on with the following instructions.

Day 4

The child's missed words on the pretest are now the words that the child needs to study. Teach your child to have good study habits. Use this formula:

(1) Look at the word. Say it.
(2) Close your eyes and spell the word. Check to see if you are correct. If not, start over.
(3) Cover the word and write it. Check to see if you are correct. If not, start over.
(4) Repeat this procedure three times for each word missed on the pretest.

Day 5

Repeat the study process for each word. Taking the child's pretest list, give the child a final written test on the words missed on the pretest. When taking the final test, require the child to write the word in a sentence. Words missed on the final test are automatically added to the next lesson.

Level 4, Numbers 17–18

Day 1

Introduce the spelling words. Have the child say each word.

Hand the child the pretest sheet so that he can see this week's spelling words. Ask the child to explain the meaning of each word.

The words in this lesson emphasize two areas. Number 17 trains the child to spell words that are accented on the penult (the next to the last syllable of the word). Number 18 deals with words that are trisyllables and contain short vowels. To introduce these words, divide the words into syllables, accenting the correct syllable, and requiring diacritical marks for each word. Diacritical markings and syllabication are all done for you in the Master Spelling List. Use the words in a sentence in context.

Day 2

Activity: Have the student write sentences using the spelling words. Give special praise every time two words are used in one sentence.

Day 3

Give the child the pretest. Find the correct word list in your master spelling list and call out the words for the child to spell, one at a time. If the child can spell every word correctly, discontinue this lesson (the child is successful) and go on to the next lesson. If the child misses any word or combination of words, continue on with the following instructions.

Day 4

The child's missed words on the pretest are now the words that the child needs to study. Teach your child to have good study habits. Use this formula:

(1) Look at the word. Say it.
(2) Close your eyes and spell the word. Check to see if you are correct. If not, start over.

(3) Cover the word and write it. Check to see if you are correct. If not, start over.
(4) Repeat this procedure three times for each word missed on the pretest.

Day 5

Repeat the study process for each word. Taking the child's pretest list, give the child a final written test on the words missed on the pretest. When taking the final test, require the child to write the word in a sentence. Words missed on the final test are automatically added to the next lesson.

Level 4, Numbers 19–20

Day 1

Introduce the spelling words. Have the child say each word.

Hand the child the pretest sheet so that he can see this week's spelling words. Ask the child to explain the meaning of each word.

This lesson deals with more homophones. The child should be capable of spelling and describing the meaning of each word. He should also be capable of using the words in a sentence in context. If he can do this, progress to the next lesson. If not, continue with the following directives.

Day 2

Activity: Play the **Party Game.** To begin, set the stage by verbally describing a party. Tell who is having the party, where the party is, and who is coming. Beginning with the first word of the spelling list, have the student tell something that happened at the party. For example, "All of the party guests ran to the picture window to see the *hart* on the lawn."

Day 3

Give the child the pretest. Find the correct word list in your master spelling list and call out the words for the child to spell, one at a time. If the child can spell every word correctly, discontinue this lesson (the child is successful) and go on to the next lesson. If the child misses any word or combination of words, continue on with the following instructions.

Day 4

The child's missed words on the pretest are now the words that the child needs to study. Teach your child to have good study habits. Use this formula:

   (1) Look at the word. Say it.
   (2) Close your eyes and spell the word. Check to see if you are correct. If not, start over.
   (3) Cover the word and write it. Check to see if you are correct. If not, start over.
   (4) Repeat this procedure three times for each word missed on the pretest.

Day 5

Repeat the study process for each word. Taking the child's pretest list, give the child a final written test on the words missed on the pretest. When taking the final test, require the child to write the word in a sentence. Words missed on the final test are automatically added to the next lesson.

Level 4, Numbers 21–22

Day 1

Introduce the spelling words. Have the child say each word.

Hand the child the pretest sheet so that he can see this week's spelling words. Ask the child to explain the meaning of each word.

This lesson trains the child to carefully observe the last syllable of the word. Number 21 contains words wherein the vowel within the last syllable is silent. Number 22 contains words wherein the vowel in the last syllable is not silent. Introduce the words by dividing each word into syllables and properly marking each vowel. Diacritical markings and syllabication are all done for you in the Master Spelling List. Use the words in a sentence in context.

Day 2

Activity: After the child has divided each word into syllables and marked each vowel with the proper diacritical mark, play the game *Association*. To play, state a word associated with a spelling word. If you were using the word **crayon**, you may want to give the associated word **color** or **draw**.

Day 3

Give the child the pretest. Find the correct word list in your master spelling list and call out the words for the child to spell, one at a time. If the child can spell every word correctly, discontinue this lesson (the child is successful) and go on to the next lesson. If the child misses any word or combination of words, continue on with the following instructions.

Day 4

The child's missed words on the pretest are now the words that the child needs to study. Teach your child to have good study habits. Use this formula:

    (1) Look at the word. Say it.
    (2) Close your eyes and spell the word. Check to see if you are correct. If not, start over.
    (3) Cover the word and write it. Check to see if you are correct. If not, start over.
    (4) Repeat this procedure three times for each word missed on the pretest.

Day 5

Repeat the study process for each word. Taking the child's pretest list, give the child a final written test on the words missed on the pretest. When taking the final test, require the child to write the word in a sentence. Words missed on the final test are automatically added to the next lesson.

Level 4, Numbers 23–25

Day 1

Since there are three sheets of words, you may choose to divide this lesson to cover two weeks.

Introduce the spelling words. Have the child say each word.

Hand the child the pretest sheet so that he can see this week's spelling words. Ask the child to explain the meaning of each word.

This lesson begins with words that have the long vowel sound (Number 23) and continues with words that end in the digraph *ow* with the long *o* sound (Number 24). Number 25 concentrates on the *"i before e except after c"* spelling rule. Use the words in a sentence in context.

Day 2

Activity: A **REBUS** is a puzzle consisting of pictures and words combined to make a story. Have the student write a story in rebus form, using at least ten spelling words.

Day 3

Give the child the pretest. Find the correct word list in your master spelling list and call out the words for the child to spell, one at a time. If the child can spell every word correctly, discontinue this lesson (the child is successful) and go on to the next lesson. If the child misses any word or combination of words, continue on with the following instructions.

Day 4

The child's missed words on the pretest are now the words that the child needs to study. Teach your child to have good study habits. Use this formula:

(1) Look at the word. Say it.
(2) Close your eyes and spell the word. Check to see if you are correct. If not, start over.
(3) Cover the word and write it. Check to see if you are correct. If not, start over.
(4) Repeat this procedure three times for each word missed on the pretest.

Day 5

Repeat the study process for each word. Taking the child's pretest list, give the child a final written test on the words missed on the pretest. When taking the final test, require the child to write the word in a sentence. Words missed on the final test are automatically added to the next lesson.

Level 4, Numbers 26–31

Day 1

Since there are six sheets of words, you may choose to divide this lesson to cover two weeks.

Introduce the spelling words. Have the child say each word.

Hand the child the pretest sheet so that he can see this week's spelling words. Ask the child to explain the meaning of each word.

This lesson consists of a review of homophones (extremely easy words to spell) and a combination of miscellaneous words. Be certain that the student can tell the difference between the meaning and spelling of the homophones before progressing to the spelling of the miscellaneous words. There are extra words within this lesson. This is intentional. We want to challenge the student to stretch his performance level. Use the words in a sentence in context.

Day 2

Activity: Use a simple drill technique to reinforce the words.

Day 3

Give the child the pretest. Find the correct word list in your master spelling list and call out the words for the child to spell, one at a time. If the child can spell every word correctly, discontinue this lesson (the child is successful) and go on to the next lesson. If the child misses any word or combination of words, continue on with the following instructions.

Day 4

The child's missed words on the pretest are now the words that the child needs to study. Teach your child to have good study habits. Use this formula:

    (1) Look at the word. Say it.
    (2) Close your eyes and spell the word. Check to see if you are correct. If not, start over.
    (3) Cover the word and write it. Check to see if you are correct. If not, start over.
    (4) Repeat this procedure three times for each word missed on the pretest.

Day 5

Repeat the study process for each word. Taking the child's pretest list, give the child a final written test on the words missed on the pretest. When taking the final test, require the child to write the word in a sentence. Words missed on the final test are automatically added to the next lesson.

Level 4, Numbers 32–33

Day 1

Introduce the spelling words. Have the child say each word.

Hand the child the pretest sheet so that he can see this week's spelling words. Ask the child to explain the meaning of each word.

The first page of this week's lesson concentrates on the various sounds of the vowels *o* and *u*. The second page concentrates on the short sound of the vowels. Introduce the words by dividing each word into syllables and marking each vowel diacritically. Diacritical markings and syllabication are all done for you in the Master Spelling List. Use the words in a sentence in context.

Day 2

Activity: After the child has divided each word into syllables and marked the vowels in each word with a diacritical mark, play the game *Word Change*. To play, write a spelling word on the board. How can the word be changed to make another word, using only the first syllable? Example: ***tribute*** may be changed to ***tribal, tribune,*** or ***tributary.***

Day 3

Give the child the pretest. Find the correct word list in your master spelling list and call out the words for the child to spell, one at a time. If the child can spell every word correctly, discontinue this lesson (the child is successful) and go on to the next lesson. If the child misses any word or combination of words, continue on with the following instructions.

Day 4

The child's missed words on the pretest are now the words that the child needs to study. Teach your child to have good study habits. Use this formula:

(1) Look at the word. Say it.
(2) Close your eyes and spell the word. Check to see if you are correct. If not, start over.

(3) Cover the word and write it. Check to see if you are correct. If not, start over.

(4) Repeat this procedure three times for each word missed on the pretest.

Day 5

Repeat the study process for each word. Taking the child's pretest list, give the child a final written test on the words missed on the pretest. When taking the final test, require the child to write the word in a sentence. Words missed on the final test are automatically added to the next lesson.

Day 1

Due to the volume of words, you may wish to teach these lessons over a two week time period. Divide the list according to the ability of the student.

Introduce the spelling words. Have the child say each word.

Hand the child the pretest sheet so that he can see this week's spelling words. Ask the child to explain the meaning of each word.

This lesson begins with homophones (extremely simple words to spell). Be sure that your child can explain the meaning of each word and spell the word before progressing. Numbers 35–37 contains miscellaneous spelling words. Have the child divide each word into syllables and mark each vowel with the proper diacritical mark. Diacritical markings and syllabication are all done for you in the Master Spelling List. Use the words in a sentence in context.

Day 2

Activity: Drill the child's spelling of these words by saying the word and then requiring the child to spell the word verbally.

Day 3

Give the child the pretest. Find the correct word list in your master spelling list and call out the words for the child to spell, one at a time. If the child can spell every word correctly, discontinue this lesson (the child is successful) and go on to the next lesson. If the child misses any word or combination of words, continue on with the following instructions.

Day 4

The child's missed words on the pretest are now the words that the child needs to study. Teach your child to have good study habits. Use this formula:

(1) Look at the word. Say it.
(2) Close your eyes and spell the word. Check to see if you are correct. If not, start over.

(3) Cover the word and write it. Check to see if you are correct. If not, start over.

(4) Repeat this procedure three times for each word missed on the pretest.

Day 5

Repeat the study process for each word. Taking the child's pretest list, give the child a final written test on the words missed on the pretest. When taking the final test, require the child to write the word in a sentence. Words missed on the final test are automatically added to the next lesson.

Level 4, Numbers 38–39

Day 1

Introduce the spelling words. Have the child say each word.

Hand the child the pretest sheet so that he can see this week's spelling words. Ask the child to explain the meaning of each word.

As children progress in spelling, more and more of the spelling words become miscellaneous words. These words do not have any pattern for spelling. They are a mixture of spelling and phonic rules. This is true of this week's spelling. To introduce the words, require the words be broken into syllables and the proper diacritical marks placed above the vowels within the words. Accent the correct syllable. Diacritical markings and syllabication are all done for you in the Master Spelling List. Use the words in a sentence in context.

Day 2

Activity: Play the game **Word Burst**. Choose one of the spelling words. Give the student ten minutes to write as many words as possible, using only the letters from the spelling word. Example: *subterfuge* = sub, rubber, butter, free.

Day 3

Give the child the pretest. Find the correct word list in your master spelling list and call out the words for the child to spell, one at a time. If the child can spell every word correctly, discontinue this lesson (the child is successful) and go on to the next lesson. If the child misses any word or combination of words, continue on with the following instructions.

Day 4

The child's missed words on the pretest are now the words that the child needs to study. Teach your child to have good study habits. Use this formula:

(1) Look at the word. Say it.
(2) Close your eyes and spell the word. Check to see if you are correct. If not, start over.

(3) Cover the word and write it. Check to see if you are correct. If not, start over.

(4) Repeat this procedure three times for each word missed on the pretest.

Day 5

Repeat the study process for each word. Taking the child's pretest list, give the child a final written test on the words missed on the pretest. When taking the final test, require the child to write the word in a sentence. Words missed on the final test are automatically added to the next lesson.

Level 4, Numbers 40–42

Day 1

Since there are three sheets of words, you may choose to divide this lesson to cover two weeks.

Introduce the spelling words. Have the child say each word.

Hand the child the pretest sheet so that he can see this week's spelling words. Ask the child to explain the meaning of each word.

Use the words in a sentence in context. The words within this lesson are miscellaneous words. Require that the child divide each word into syllables, mark the vowel with its proper diacritical mark, and accent the correct syllable.

Day 2

Activity: Drill the words verbally. If this type of drill is not effective, have the child write each word five or ten times.

Day 3

Give the child the pretest. Find the correct word list in your master spelling list and call out the words for the child to spell, one at a time. If the child can spell every word correctly, discontinue this lesson (the child is successful) and go on to the next lesson. If the child misses any word or combination of words, continue on with the following instructions.

Day 4

The child's missed words on the pretest are now the words that the child needs to study. Teach your child to have good study habits. Use this formula:

    (1) Look at the word. Say it.
    (2) Close your eyes and spell the word. Check to see if you are correct. If not, start over.
    (3) Cover the word and write it. Check to see if you are correct. If not, start over.
    (4) Repeat this procedure three times for each word missed on the pretest.

Day 5

Repeat the study process for each word. Taking the child's pretest list, give the child a final written test on the words missed on the pretest. When taking the final test, require the child to write the word in a sentence. Words missed on the final test are automatically added to the next lesson.

Level 4, Numbers 43–46

Day 1

Due to the volume of words, you may wish to teach these lessons over a two week time period. Divide the list according to the ability of the student.

Introduce the spelling words. Have the child say each word.

Hand the child the pretest sheet so that he can see this week's spelling words. Ask the child to explain the meaning of each word.

Use the words in a sentence in context. This lesson contains miscellaneous words, interspersed with one page of homophones. Require each word to be broken into syllables, the vowels to be diacritically marked, and the syllables accented correctly.

Day 2

Activity: Write sentences, using the spelling words. Try to use as many words as possible in one sentence. For example, "A **buffoon** was seen to **disturb** the **inert gate** though the **great gate** expert from **Greece** thought it was **absurd**."

Day 3

Give the child the pretest. Find the correct word list in your master spelling list and call out the words for the child to spell, one at a time. If the child can spell every word correctly, discontinue this lesson (the child is successful) and go on to the next lesson. If the child misses any word or combination of words, continue on with the following instructions.

Day 4

The child's missed words on the pretest are now the words that the child needs to study. Teach your child to have good study habits. Use this formula:

(1) Look at the word. Say it.
(2) Close your eyes and spell the word. Check to see if you are correct. If not, start over.

(3) Cover the word and write it. Check to see if you are correct. If not, start over.

(4) Repeat this procedure three times for each word missed on the pretest.

Day 5

Repeat the study process for each word. Taking the child's pretest list, give the child a final written test on the words missed on the pretest. When taking the final test, require the child to write the word in a sentence. Words missed on the final test are automatically added to the next lesson.

Level 4, Numbers 47–50

Day 1

Due to the volume of words, you may wish to teach these lessons over a two week time period. Divide the list according to the ability of the student.

Introduce the spelling words. Have the child say each word.

Hand the child the pretest sheet so that he can see this week's spelling words. Ask the child to explain the meaning of each word.

The words within this lesson are miscellaneous words. Require that the child divide each word into syllables, mark each vowel with its proper diacritical mark, and accent the proper syllable. Diacritical markings and syllabication are all done for you in the Master Spelling List. Use the words in a sentence in context.

Day 2

Activity: Use any form of drill that is effective.

Day 3

Give the child the pretest. Find the correct word list in your master spelling list and call out the words for the child to spell, one at a time. If the child can spell every word correctly, discontinue this lesson (the child is successful) and go on to the next lesson. If the child misses any word or combination of words, continue on with the following instructions.

Day 4

The child's missed words on the pretest are now the words that the child needs to study. Teach your child to have good study habits. Use this formula:

(1) Look at the word. Say it.
(2) Close your eyes and spell the word. Check to see if you are correct. If not, start over.

(3) Cover the word and write it. Check to see if you are correct. If not, start over.

(4) Repeat this procedure three times for each word missed on the pretest.

Day 5

Repeat the study process for each word. Taking the child's pretest list, give the child a final written test on the words missed on the pretest. When taking the final test, require the child to write the word in a sentence. Words missed on the final test are automatically added to the next lesson.

Level 4, Numbers 51–52

Day 1

Introduce the spelling words. Have the child say each word.

Hand the child the pretest sheet so that he can see this week's spelling words. Ask the child to explain the meaning of each word.

This lesson contains one page (Number 51) of words that are accented on the first syllable, and one page (Number 52) of words that are monosyllables. Since syllables are emphasized, require the student break each word into syllables. Have the student explain which syllabication rule applies to the first syllable. Syllabication rules are listed in the introduction to this book. Your Master Spelling List gives you the correct syllabication for each word. Use the words in a sentence in context.

Day 2

Activity: Obtain a game of *Scrabble*. Play with the spelling pretests on the table. Give triple points for every spelling word used.

Day 3

Give the child the pretest. Find the correct word list in your master spelling list and call out the words for the child to spell, one at a time. If the child can spell every word correctly, discontinue this lesson (the child is successful) and go on to the next lesson. If the child misses any word or combination of words, continue on with the following instructions.

Day 4

The child's missed words on the pretest are now the words that the child needs to study. Teach your child to have good study habits. Use this formula:

(1) Look at the word. Say it.
(2) Close your eyes and spell the word. Check to see if you are correct. If not, start over.
(3) Cover the word and write it. Check to see if you are correct. If not, start over.
(4) Repeat this procedure three times for each word missed on the pretest.

Day 5

Repeat the study process for each word. Taking the child's pretest list, give the child a final written test on the words missed on the pretest. When taking the final test, require the child to write the word in a sentence. Words missed on the final test are automatically added to the next lesson.

Level 4, Numbers 53–54

Day 1

Introduce the spelling words. Have the child say each word.

Hand the child the pretest sheet so that he can see this week's spelling words. Ask the child to explain the meaning of each word.

This lesson concentrates on miscellaneous spelling words. Use the words in a sentence in context.

Day 2

Activity: Use any type of drill which is successful for your student.

Day 3

Give the child the pretest. Find the correct word list in your master spelling list and call out the words for the child to spell, one at a time. If the child can spell every word correctly, discontinue this lesson (the child is successful) and go on to the next lesson. If the child misses any word or combination of words, continue on with the following instructions.

Day 4

The child's missed words on the pretest are now the words that the child needs to study. Teach your child to have good study habits. Use this formula:

(1) Look at the word. Say it.
(2) Close your eyes and spell the word. Check to see if you are correct. If not, start over.
(3) Cover the word and write it. Check to see if you are correct. If not, start over.
(4) Repeat this procedure three times for each word missed on the pretest.

Day 5

Repeat the study process for each word. Taking the child's pretest list, give the child a final written test on the words missed on the pretest. When taking the final test, require the child to write the word in a sentence. Words missed on the final test are automatically added to the next lesson.

Level 4, Numbers 55–58

Day 1

Since there are four sheets of words, you may choose to divide this lesson to cover two weeks.

Introduce the spelling words. Have the child say each word.

Hand the child the pretest sheet so that he can see this week's spelling words. Ask the child to explain the meaning of each word.

This lesson consists of miscellaneous words and homophones. Use the words in a sentence in context.

Day 2

Activity: Play the game *Vowel Search*. At a GO signal from you, have the child count the number of vowels that are long. After a time lapse of one minute, conclude the game. How many vowels did the student find? The section on DIACRITICAL MARKS in the introduction explains the vowel sounds. Check your Master Spelling List for the diacritical markings for each word.

Day 3

Give the child the pretest. Find the correct word list in your master spelling list and call out the words for the child to spell, one at a time. If the child can spell every word correctly, discontinue this lesson (the child is successful) and go on to the next lesson. If the child misses any word or combination of words, continue on with the following instructions.

Day 4

The child's missed words on the pretest are now the words that the child needs to study. Teach your child to have good study habits. Use this formula:

(1) Look at the word. Say it.
(2) Close your eyes and spell the word. Check to see if you are correct. If not, start over.

(3) Cover the word and write it. Check to see if you are correct. If not, start over.

(4) Repeat this procedure three times for each word missed on the pretest.

Day 5

Repeat the study process for each word. Taking the child's pretest list, give the child a final written test on the words missed on the pretest. When taking the final test, require the child to write the word in a sentence. Words missed on the final test are automatically added to the next lesson.

Level 4, Numbers 59–60

Day 1

Introduce the spelling words. Have the child say each word.

Hand the child the pretest sheet so that he can see this week's spelling words. Ask the child to explain the meaning of each word.

This lesson contains diverse sounds. Number 59 deals with words wherein the *i* sounds like the consonant *y*. Number 60 contains words which have *ng* in the spelling of the word, but sound as if the *g* were doubled when pronounced. Use the words in a sentence in context.

Day 2

Activity: Play *Word Race*. On a board, write the first two letters of a word within the spelling list. See how quickly the student can guess what the word is.

Day 3

Give the child the pretest. Find the correct word list in your master spelling list and call out the words for the child to spell, one at a time. If the child can spell every word correctly, discontinue this lesson (the child is successful) and go on to the next lesson. If the child misses any word or combination of words, continue on with the following instructions.

Day 4

The child's missed words on the pretest are now the words that the child needs to study. Teach your child to have good study habits. Use this formula:

(1) Look at the word. Say it.
(2) Close your eyes and spell the word. Check to see if you are correct. If not, start over.
(3) Cover the word and write it. Check to see if you are correct. If not, start over.
(4) Repeat this procedure three times for each word missed on the pretest.

Day 5

Repeat the study process for each word. Taking the child's pretest list, give the child a final written test on the words missed on the pretest. When taking the final test, require the child to write the word in a sentence. Words missed on the final test are automatically added to the next lesson.

Level 4, Numbers 61–62

Day 1

Introduce the spelling words. Have the child say each word.

Hand the child the pretest sheet so that he can see this week's spelling words. Ask the child to explain the meaning of each word.

The first section of words (Number 61) in this lesson highlight words in which the *s* in the word sounds like *sh* as in the word **sure**. Number 62 deals with words which have *se* as an ending. Use the words in a sentence in context.

Day 2

Activity: Drill the words in a manner which is most successful for the student.

Day 3

Give the child the pretest. Find the correct word list in your master spelling list and call out the words for the child to spell, one at a time. If the child can spell every word correctly, discontinue this lesson (the child is successful) and go on to the next lesson. If the child misses any word or combination of words, continue on with the following instructions.

Day 4

The child's missed words on the pretest are now the words that the child needs to study. Teach your child to have good study habits. Use this formula:

    (1) Look at the word. Say it.
    (2) Close your eyes and spell the word. Check to see if you are correct. If not, start over.
    (3) Cover the word and write it. Check to see if you are correct. If not, start over.
    (4) Repeat this procedure three times for each word missed on the pretest.

Day 5

Repeat the study process for each word. Taking the child's pretest list, give the child a final written test on the words missed on the pretest. When taking the final test, require the child to write the word in a sentence. Words missed on the final test are automatically added to the next lesson.

Level 4, Numbers 63–64

Day 1

Introduce the spelling words. Have the child say each word.

Hand the child the pretest sheet so that he can see this week's spelling words. Ask the child to explain the meaning of each word.

The words within this lesson are random in placement. Introduce the words by illustrating the syllabication of each word, diacritical marking of the vowels, and accented syllables. Your Master Spelling List gives you the correct syllabication and diacritical markings for each word. Use the words in a sentence in context.

Day 2

Activity: Play *Telegrams*. In this game, a word is separated into individual letters, with each letter being the first letter of a word in a telegram sent to a friend. For example, the word *elaborate* might be made into the telegram as follows: *Eeeeek! Larry And Barbara Ordered Rare Aardvark To Eat!*

Day 3

Give the child the pretest. Find the correct word list in your master spelling list and call out the words for the child to spell, one at a time. If the child can spell every word correctly, discontinue this lesson (the child is successful) and go on to the next lesson. If the child misses any word or combination of words, continue on with the following instructions.

Day 4

The child's missed words on the pretest are now the words that the child needs to study. Teach your child to have good study habits. Use this formula:

    (1) Look at the word. Say it.
    (2) Close your eyes and spell the word. Check to see if you are correct. If not, start over.
    (3) Cover the word and write it. Check to see if you are correct. If not, start over.
    (4) Repeat this procedure three times for each word missed on the pretest.

Day 5

Repeat the study process for each word. Taking the child's pretest list, give the child a final written test on the words missed on the pretest. When taking the final test, require the child to write the word in a sentence. Words missed on the final test are automatically added to the next lesson.

Level 4, Numbers 65–66

Day 1

Introduce the spelling words. Have the child say each word.

Hand the child the pretest sheet so that he can see this week's spelling words. Ask the child to explain the meaning of each word.

The words within this lesson are random in their appearance. Have the child syllabicate, diacritically mark, and accent each word. The child should be well versed in this practice by this time. Use the words in a sentence in context.

Day 2

Activity: Play the game *Eagle Eye*. Taking each word on the spelling list, have the student look at the word to identify the root of the word (when applicable). The word *dogmatical*, for example, has the root word *dogma* within it. If neither you nor your child know the root to a word, pass on to one you do. This is only an introductory practice in root words. Root words are studied in detail in Level 6 of Success In Spelling.

Day 3

Give the child the pretest. Find the correct word list in your master spelling list and call out the words for the child to spell, one at a time. If the child can spell every word correctly, discontinue this lesson (the child is successful) and go on to the next lesson. If the child misses any word or combination of words, continue on with the following instructions.

Day 4

The child's missed words on the pretest are now the words that the child needs to study. Teach your child to have good study habits. Use this formula:

    (1) Look at the word. Say it.
    (2) Close your eyes and spell the word. Check to see if you are correct. If not, start over.
    (3) Cover the word and write it. Check to see if you are correct. If not, start over.
    (4) Repeat this procedure three times for each word missed on the pretest.

Day 5

Repeat the study process for each word. Taking the child's pretest list, give the child a final written test on the words missed on the pretest. When taking the final test, require the child to write the word in a sentence. Words missed on the final test are automatically added to the next lesson.

MASTER SPELLING LIST

Level 4 #1

raised	rāiṣed
razed	rāzed
pray	prāy
prey	prey
pore	pōre
pour	pōur
please	plēaṣe
pleas	plēaṣ
bell	bell
belle	belle
plumb	plumb (plum)
plum	plum

Level 4 #2

board	bōard
bored	bōred
blue	blūe
blew	blew
piece	piēce
peace	pēace
new	new
knew	knew (nū)
gnu	gnū (nū)
arc	ärc
ark	ärk

Level 4 #3

abrupt	a brupt'
construct	cŏn struct'
annul	an nul'
instruct	in struct'
intrust	in trust'
discuss	dis cuss'
deduct	dē duct'
result	rē ṣult'
across	à crọss'
adopt	à dopt'
belong	bē long'
agree	à gree'

Level 4 #4

asleep	à sleep'
decree	dē cree'
esteem	es teem'
degree	dē gree'
attire	at fīre'
entice	en fīce'
entire	en fīre'
incline	in clīne'
incite	in cīte'
invite	in vīte'
oblige	ō blīġe'
perspire	pẽr spīre'

Level 4 #5

contact	con' tact
hobby	hob' by
forest	for' est
lofty	lọft' y
nostril	nos' tril
product	prod' uct
problem	prob' lem
torrent	tor' rent
huddle	hud' dle
public	pub' lic
pungent	pun' ġent
publish	pub' lish

Level 4 #6

cadence	cā' dence
pavement	pāve' ment
native	nā' tive
equal	ē' quăl.
freedom	free' dŏm
meeting	meet' ing
Friday	Frī' dāy
migrate	mī' grāte
tribal	trīb' ăl
crisis	crī' sis
hydrant	hȳ' drănt
silent	sī' lent

MASTER SPELLING LIST

Level 4 #7

beard	bēard
eaves	ēaves
crease	crēase
heave	hēave
leap	lēap
knee	knee (nē)
spleen	spleen
frank	frañk
smack	smack
clamp	clamp
build	build (bild)
built	built

Level 4 #8

walk	walk (wak)
lawn	lawn
chalk	chalk (chak)
fault	fault
spawn	spawn
drift	drift
fund	fund
verse	vẽrse
search	sẽarch
fern	fẽrn
serve	sẽrve
were	wẽre

Level 4 #9

ennoble	en nō′ ble
elopement	ē lōpe′ ment
exponent	ex pō′ nent
heroic	hē rō′ ic
detachment	dē tach′ ment
dogmatic	dog mat′ ic
dramatic	drȧ mat′ ic
ecstatic	ec stat′ ic
elastic	ē las′ tic
inducement	in dūce′ ment
acumen	ȧ cū′ men

Level 4 #10

accusing	ac cūṣ′ ing
amusement	ȧ mūṣe′ ment
allurement	al lūre′ ment
establish	es tab′ lish
fanatic	fȧ nat′ ic
fantastic	fan tas′ tic
gigantic	ğī gan′ tic
inhabit	in hab′ it
abusive	ȧ bū′ sive
perusal	pē ruṣ′ ăl
pursuant	pūr sū′ ănt
refusal	rē fūṣ′ ăl

Level 4 #11

sulfuric	sul fū′ ric
assemblage	as sem′ blāġe
appendix	ap pen′ dix
attendant	at tend′ ănt
intestate	in tes′ tāte
compensate	com′ pen sāte
strait	strāit
straight	strāight
rote	rōte
wrote	wrōte
wave	wāve
waive	wāive

Level 4 #12

boll	bōll
bowl	bōwl
nose	nōṣe
knows	knōwṣ (nōs)
rein	rein
rain	rāin
reign	reign
paws	pawṣ
pause	pauṣe
pride	prĭde
pried	prĭed

MASTER SPELLING LIST

Level 4 #13

afloat	à flōat′
bemoan	bē mōan′
below	bē lōw′
bestow	bē stōw′
deplore	dē plōre′
postpone	pōst pōne′
discourse	dis′ cōurse
deport	dē pōrt′
remote	rē mōte′
dilute	di lūte′
ensue	en sūe′
demure	dē mūre′

Level 4 #14

abreast	à breast′
befriend	bē friend′
ahead	à head′
behead	bē head′
attempt	at tempt′
distress	dis tress′
amidst	à midst′
eclipse	ē clipse′
extinct	ex tiñct′
forgive	fǫr give′
inflect	in flect′
inflict	in flict′

Level 4 #15

austere	ạus tēre′
revere	rē vēre′
bequeath	bē quēath′
beseech	bē seech′
decrease	dē crēase′
increase	in crēase′
demean	dē mēan′
repeal	rē pēal′
appeal	ap pēal′
appear	ap pēar′
appease	ap pēase′
blaspheme	blàs phēme′

Level 4 #16

discreet	dis creet′
extreme	ex trēme′
entreat	en trēat′
impeach	im pēach′
awry	à wrȳ′
beguile	bē guīle′
deprive	dē prīve′
describe	dē scrībe′
despise	dē spīṣe′
prescribe	prē scrībe′
decline	dē clīne′
requite	rē quīte′

Level 4 #17

domestic	dō mes′ tic
embezzle	em bez′ zle
embellish	em bel′ lish
parental	pà ren′ tăl
poetic	pō et′ ic
presented	prē sent′ ed
preventive	prē vent′ ive
refreshing	rē fresh′ ing
replenish	rē plen′ ish
surrender	sur ren′ dĕr
redundant	rē dun′ dănt
concurrent	cǒn cūr′ rent

Level 4 #18

abolish	à bol′ ish
accomplish	ac com′ plish
abhorrent	ab hǫr′ rent
admonish	ad mon′ ish
allotment	al lot′ ment
colossus	cō los′ sus
demolish	dē mol′ ish
harmonic	här mon′ ic
imposter	im pos′ ter
laconic	là con′ ic
apostate	à pos′ tāte
embody	em bod′ y

MASTER SPELLING LIST

Level 4 #19

hart	härt
heart	heärt
hear	hēar
here	hēre
heard	hĕard
herd	hĕrd
him	him
hymn	hymn (him)
hole	hōle
whole	whōle (hōl)
hour	hour (our)
our	our

Level 4 #20

in	in
inn	inn
key	kēy
quay	quay
rhyme	rhȳme
rime	rīme
knot	knot (not)
not	not
know	knōw (nō)
no	nō
hi	hī
high	hīgh (hī)

Level 4 #21

gladden	glad′ den
ravel	rav′ el
happen	hap′ pen
sadden	sad′ den
freshen	fresh′ en
open	ō′ pen
lengthen	length′ en
quicken	quick′ en
written	writ′ ten (rit′)
glisten	glis′ ten
drunken	druñk′ en
mutton	mut′ tŏn

Level 4 #22

crayon	crāy′ ŏn
omen	ō′ men
siphon	sī′ phŏn
barrel	bar′ rel
parcel	pär′ cel
aspen	asp′ en
cabin	cab′ in
dragon	drag′ ŏn
gravel	grav′ el
bevel	bev′ el
sudden	sud′ den
lemon	lem′ ŏn

Level 4 #23

credence	crē′ dence
fracas	frā′ căs
greedy	greed′ y
gateway	gāte′ wāy
namesake	nāme′ sāke
measles	mēa′ ṣleṣ
people	pēo′ ple
legion	lē′ giŏn
region	rē′ ġiŏn
steeple	stee′ ple
cipher	cī′ phẽr
highland	hīgh′ lănd

Level 4 #24

arrow	ar′ rōw
narrow	nar′ rōw
harrow	har′ rōw
sparrow	spar′ rōw
shallow	shal′ lōw
shadow	shad′ ōw
mellow	mel′ lōw
meadow	mead′ ōw
window	win′ dōw
widow	wid′ ōw
borrow	bor′ rōw
fallow	fal′ lōw

MASTER SPELLING LIST

Level 4 #25

grieve	grĭĕve
retrieve	rē trĭĕve′
thieve	thĭĕve
relief	rē lĭēf′
achieving	à chĭēv′ ing
relieve	rē lĭēve′
believe	bē lĭēve′
pieced	pĭēced
conceit	cŏn cēit′
deceitful	dē cēit′ fụl
sheik	shēik

Level 4 #26

bald	bäld
bawled	bạwled
bear	beãr
bare	bãre
be	bē
bee	bee
air	ãir
ere	ere (ãr)
eʹer	eʹer (ãr)
heir	heir (ãr)
aisle	aīsle (īl)
isle	īsle (īl)

Level 4 #27

clever	clev′ ẽr
wayward	wāy′ wărd
painter	pāint′ ẽr
digest	dĭ′ ġest
lightning	lĭght′ ning
portrait	pōr′ trāit
novice	nov′ ice
climate	clĭ′ māte
scaffold	scaf′ fŏld
transcript	tran′ script
menace	men′ ăce
shepherd	shep′ hẽrd

Level 4 #28

wholesome	whōle′ sŏme
button	but′ tŏn
jostle	jos′ tle (-l)
picnic	pic′ nic
grumble	grum′ ble
trouble	troub′ le
sarcasm	sär′ casm
tarnish	tär′ nish
relapse	rē lapse′
profess	prō fess′
revenge	rē venge′
flighty	flĭght′ y

Level 4 #29

educate	ed′ ū cāte
effigy	ef′ fi ġy
ebony	eb′ ŏn y
elephant	el′ ē phănt
embassy	em′ băs sy
exodus	ex′ ō dus
felony	fel′ ŏ ny
genesis	ġen′ e sis
federal	fed′ ẽr ăl
penitent	pen′ i tent
fellowship	fel′ lōw ship
resident	res i dent

Level 4 #30

bail	bāil
bale	bāle
base	bāse
bass	bāss
beach	bēach
beech	beech
beat	bēat
beet	beet
bin	bin
been	been (bin)
bold	bōld
bowled	bōwled

MASTER SPELLING LIST

Level 4 #31

berth	bĕrth
birth	bĭrth
cast	c̠àst
caste	c̠àste
cede	c̠ede
seed	seed
coarse	c̠ōarse
course	c̠ourse
cane	c̠āne
Cain	C̠āin
wry	wrȳ
rye	rȳe

Level 4 #32

tonnage	tŏn' năg̠e
worry	wŏr' ry
wonder	wŏn' dĕr
novel	nov' el
booty	bo̤o̤' ty
movement	möve' ment
stucco	stuc̠' c̠ō
buzzard	buz' zărd
custard	c̠us' tărd
hundred	hun' dred
husband	hus̠' bănd
buckle	buck' le (-l)

Level 4 #33

reptile	rep' tile
sentence	sen' tence
refuse	rēf ūse'
speckle	spec̠k' le
sterile	ster' ile
Wednesday	Wednes' dāy (wenz')
zealous	zeal' ous
dictate	dic̠' tāte
pillage	pil' lăg̠e
tribute	trib' ute
bramble	bram' ble
callous	c̠al' lous

Level 4 #34

cell	cell
sell	sell
cent	cent
sent	sent
scent	scent
chased	chāsed (chāst)
chaste	chāste
clause	clau̟se
claws	claw̟s
cord	cord
chord	chord

Level 4 #35

conceal	c̠ŏn cēal'
absolve	ab solve'
congeal	c̠ŏn g̠ēal'
dissolve	dis̠ solve'
respond	rē spond'
begrudge	bē grudg̠e'
convulse	c̠ŏn vulse'
repulse	rē pulse'
indulge	in dulg̠e'
succumb	suc̠ c̠umb'
affront	af frŏnt'
among	à mŏng'

Level 4 #36

refrain	rē frāin'
restrain	rē strāin'
remain	rē māin'
retain	rē tāin'
retail	re' tāil
reprint	rē print'
restrict	rē strict'
submit	sub mit'
reproach	rē prōach'
patrol	pà trōl'
before	bē fōre'
retrace	rē trāce'

MASTER SPELLING LIST

Level 4 #37

fashion	fash′ iŏn
knapsack	knap′ sack
galley	gal′ ley
ladder	lad′ dĕr
lattice	lat′ tice (tis)
passive	pas′ sive
practice	prac̣′ tice
rapid	rap′ id
rabid	rab′ id
tactics	tac̣′ tic̣s
biscuit	bis′ c̣uit
image	im′ ăġe

Level 4 #38

alkali	al′ kȧ lĭ
asterisk	as′ tẽr isk
alkaline	al′ kȧ lĭne
bachelor	bach′ e lŏr
fabricate	fab′ ri c̄āte
galaxy	gal′ ax y
mariner	mar′ i nẽr
paragraph	par′ ȧ grȧph
paragon	par′ ȧ gon
paraphrase	par′ ȧ phrāṣe
cherubim	cher′ u̇ bim
density	den′ si ty

Level 4 #39

expedite	ex′ pē dĭte
petulant	pet′ ū lănt
pediment	ped′ i ment
pelican	pel′ i c̆ăn
recompense	rec̣′ ŏm pense
spherical	spher′ i c̆ăl
currency	c̣ur′ ren cy
subterfuge	sub′ tẽr fūġe
nullify	nul′ li fȳ
subsidy	sub sī dy′
fiftieth	fif′ ti eth
miracle	mir′ ȧ c̣le

Level 4 #40

rigorous	rig′ ŏr ous
synonym	syn′ ō nym
nimbleness	nim′ ble ness
wilderness	wil′ dĕr ness
conjugate	c̣on′ jū gāte
controvert	c̣on′ trō vẽrt
consecrate	c̣on′ sē c̣rāte
coronet	c̣or′ ō net
dominant	dom′ i nănt
arbitrate	är′ bi trāte
armament	är′ mȧ ment

Level 4 #41

decimal	dec′ i măl
emphasis	em′ phȧ sis
despotism	des′ pō tiṣm
epitaph	ep′ i taph
lethargy	leth′ ăr ġy
pentateuch	pen′ tȧ teūc̣h
metaphor	met′ ȧ phŏr
editor	ed′ i tŏr
senator	sen′ ȧ tŏr
seraphim	ser′ ȧ phim
specimen	spec′ i men
speculate	spec̣′ ū lāte

Level 4 #42

criticism	c̣rit′ i ciṣm
mystery	mys′ tẽr y
cylinder	cyl′ in dẽr
mystify	mys′ ti fȳ
physical	phyṣ′ ic̣ ăl
typify	typ′ i fȳ
judgment	judġ′ ment
common	c̣om′ mŏn
dogma	dog′ mȧ
dolphin	dol′ phin
hostile	hos′ tile
modern	mod′ ẽrn

MASTER SPELLING LIST

Level 4 #43

gage	gāġe
gauge	gāuġe
gate	gāte
gait	gait
gilt	gilt
guilt	guilt (gilt)
great	greāt
grate	grāte
grease	grēase
Greece	Greece
groan	grōan
grown	grōwn

Level 4 #44

alert	à lĕrt′
avert	à vĕrt′
assert	as sĕrt′
concern	cŏn cĕrn′
pervert	pĕr vĕrt′
expert	ex′ pĕrt
inert	in ĕrt′
infer	in fĕr′
insert	in sĕrt′
invert	in vĕrt′
prefer	prē fĕr′
subvert	sub vĕrt′

Level 4 #45

superb	sū pĕrb′
recur	rē cŭr′
absurd	ab sŭrd′
demur	dē mŭr′
disturb	dis tŭrb′
remove	rē mŏve′
aloof	à lŏof′
balloon	bal lŏon′
buffoon	buf fŏon′
avail	à vāil′
await	à wāit′
decay	dē cāy′

Level 4 #46

prevail	prē vāil′
abstain	ab stāin′
reclaim	rē clāim′
acquaint	ac quaint
assuage	as suāġe′ (-swāj′)
blockade	block āde′
display	dis plāy′
entail	en tāil′
obtain	ob tāin′
contain	cŏn tāin′
persuade	pĕr suāde′
recall	rē cạll′

Level 4 #47

alpha	al′ phȧ
damask	dam′ ăsk
bracket	brack′ et
padlock	pad′ lock
placid	plac′ id
Sabbath	Sab′ băth
stagnant	stag′ nănt
mandate	man′ dāte
stagnate	stag′ nāte
comfort	cŏm′ fŏrt
other	ŏth′ ĕr
mother	mŏth′ ĕr

Level 4 #48

legate	leg′ ăte
message	mes′ săġe
membrane	mem′ brāne
rescue	res′ cūe
flout	flout
meant	meant (ment)
quick	quick
solve	solve
wrong	wrọng
shrimp	shrimp
cause	cạuse
gauze	gạuze

MASTER SPELLING LIST

Level 4 #49

squaw	squ̲aw
afraid	à frāid′
cross	cr̲oss
contempt	c̲ŏn tempt′
command	c̲ŏm mȧnd′
commence	c̲ŏm mence′
commend	c̲ŏm mend′
complaint	c̲ŏm plāint′
approach	ap prōach′
curtail	c̲ūr′ tāil′
repute	rē pūte′
skirmish	skĭr′ mish

Level 4 #50

fervency	fẽr′ ven cy
nursery	nũrs′ ẽr y
mercury	mẽr′ c̲ū ry
perjury	pẽr′ jū ry
artery	är′ tẽr y
harmony	här′ mō ny
harmonize	här′ mō nĭze
affluent	af′ flū ent
barrier	bar′ ri ẽr
barrister	bar′ ris tẽr
carrion	c̲ar′ ri ŏn
baluster	bal′ us tẽr

Level 4 #51

flagrancy	flā′ grăn cy
radiance	rā′ di ănce
fragrance	frā′ grănce
slavery	slāv′ ẽr y
maintenance	māin′ te nănce
dialect	dĭ′ à le̲ct
diagram	dĭ′ à gram
diary	dĭ′ à ry
ivory	ĭ′ vō ry
pliable	plĭ′ à ble
pedestal	ped′ es tăl
medicine	med′ i cine

Level 4 #52

field	fiēld
fiend	fiēnd
thief	thiēf
shriek	shriēk
yield	yiēld
fierce	fiērce
pierce	piērce (pērs)
niece	niēce (nēs)
crock	c̲rock
shock	shock
mock	mock
league	lēague (lēg)

Level 4 #53

false	f̲alse
swarm	sw̲arm
quart	qu̲art
thwart	thw̲art
sought	s̲ought
bought	b̲ought (bọt) or (bout)
bright	brĭght
plight	plĭght (plĭt)
pitch	pitch
stitch	stitch
hitch	hitch
patch	patch

Level 4 #54

batch	batch
latch	latch
match	match
edge	edġe (ej)
hedge	hedġe
ledge	ledġe
wedge	wedġe
bridge	bridġe
ridge	ridġe
hinge	hinġe
cringe	c̲rinġe
bilge	bilġe

MASTER SPELLING LIST

Level 4 #55

hall	hạll
haul	hạul
hay	hāy
hey	hęy
hare	hãre
hair	hãir
heal	hēal
heel	heel
hire	hīre
higher	hīgh′ ẽr
hoop	họop
whoop	whọop

Level 4 #56

faith	fāith
strange	strānġe
scrape	sc̣rāpe
greet	greet
perch	pẽrch
champ	champ
drench	drench
squeeze	squeeze
grist	grist
shrink	shriñk
theme	thēme

Level 4 #57

chime	chīme
badge	badġe
smart	smärt
dodge	dodġe (doj)
brawl	brạwl
dwarf	dwạrf
grant	grȧnt
spunk	spuñk
length	length
launch	lạunch
pledge	pledġe
screech	sc̣reech

Level 4 #58

knight	knīght (nīt)
night	nīght (nīt)
knave	knāve (nāv)
nave	nāve
loan	lōan
lone	lōne
links	liñks
lynx	lyñx
loch	loc̣h
lock	lock
lax	lax
lacks	lacks

Level 4 #59

alien	āl′ ien (-yen)
union	ūn′ iŏn (-yun)
savior	sā viŏr
senior	sēn′ iŏr
junior	jůn′ iŏr
spaniel	span′ iel
valiant	val′ iănt
indian	in′ di ăn
onion	ŏn′ iŏn
brilliant	bril′ liănt
million	mil′ liŏn
trillion	tril′ liŏn

Level 4 #60

anger	an′ gẽr
anguish	añ′ guish
angry	añ′ gry
dangle	dañ′ gle
jingle	jiñ′ gle
mangle	mañ′ gle
wrangle	wrañ′ gle
longer	lọng′ ẽr
stronger	strọng′ ẽr
bungle	buñ′ gle
hunger	huñ′ ger
languish	lañ′ guish

MASTER SPELLING LIST

Level 4 #61

surely	sùre′ ly
sugar	sug′ ăr
sureness	sùre′ ness
censure	cen′ sùre
pressure	pres′ sùre
issue	is′ sūe (ish′ ū)
tissue	tis′ sùe (tish′ ù)
assure	as sūre′
insure	in sūre′
assurance	as sūr′ ănce
insurance	in sūr′ ănce
insurer	in sūr′ ēr

Level 4 #62

condense	cŏn dense′
dispense	dis pense′
defense	dē fense′
expense	ex pense′
incense	in cense′
immense	im mense′
offense	of fense′
pretense	prē tense′
suspense	sus pense′
license	lĭc′ ense
intense	in tense′
nonsense	non′ sense

Level 4 #63

amalgamate	à mal′ gà māte
facilitate	fà cil′ i tāte
assassinate	as sas′ si nāte
coagulate	cō ag′ ū lāte
concatenate	con cat′ e nāte
confabulate	cŏn fab′ ū lāte
congratulate	cŏn grat′ ū lāte
contaminate	cŏn tam′ i nāte
decapitate	dē cap′ i tāte
circus	cĭr′ cus
elaborate	ē lab′ ō rāte
cheese	cheese

Level 4 #64

furnace	fūr′ năce
nervous	nĕrv′ ous
furlong	fūr′ long
purchase	pūr′ chăse
surface	sūr′ făce
capacity	cà pac′ i ty
comparison	cŏm par′ i sŏn
comparative	cŏm par′ à tive
compatible	cŏm pat′ i ble
declarative	dē clar′ à tive
diagonal	dĭ ag′ ō năl
diameter	dĭ am′ e tēr

Level 4 #65

dogmatically	dog mat′ i căl ly
depravity	dē prav′ i ty
ambassador	am bas′ sà dŏr
ambient	am′ bi ent
calamine	cal′ à mīne
juvenile	jŭ′ ven ile
pedigree	ped′ i gree
register	reġ′ is tēr
revelry	rev′ el ry
skeptical	skep′ ti căl
verily	ver′ i ly
halcyon	hal′ cy ŏn

Level 4 #66

brassiere	bras sière′
graze	grāze
glazier	glā′ zĩēr
seizure	sēi′ zūre
hosiery	hō′ șiēr y
fusion	fū′ șion
azure	aẓ′ ūre
measure	meaș′ ūre
pleasure	pleaș′ ūre
evasion	ē vā′ șion
invasion	in vā′ șion
persuasion	pĕr suā′ șion

QUICKIE WORDS

Level: Grade 5 #1

appear	ap pēar′
buy	buȳ
baby	bā′ by
care	c̦āre
century	cen′ tū ry
cross	c̦ross
either	ēi′ thẽr
everything	ev′ ẽr y thing
factors	fac̦′ tŏrs
floor	flōor
hill	hill
ice	īce

Level: Grade 5 #2

jumped	jumped (jumt)
outside	out′ sīde
metal	met′ ăl
pushed	pu̧shed (pu̧sht)
result	rē su̧lt′
ride	rīde
sleep	sleep
snow	snōw
solve	solve
son	sŏn
speak	spēak
tall	ta̧ll

Level: Grade 5 #3

village	vil′ lăġe
bed	bed
already	a̧l read′ y
bright	brīght (brīt)
consonant	c̦on′ sō nănt
copy	c̦op′ y
dictionary	dic̦′ tion ār y
ease	ēa̧se
everyone	ev′ ẽr y one
free	free
hope	hōpe
instead	in stead′ (-sted′)

Level: Grade 5 #4

lake	lāke
lead	lead (led)
laughed	läughed (läft or laft)
method	meth′ ŏd
nation	nā′ tion
phrase	phrāṣe
section	sec̦′ tion
quite	quīte
soil	soil
spring	spring
temperature	tem′ pẽr à tūre
themselves	them selveṣ′

Level: Grade 5 #5

type	tȳpe
act	ac̦t
within	with in′
age	āġe
although	a̧l thōugh′
amount	à mount′
broken	brō′ ken
build	build (bild)
count	c̦ount
eat	ēat
gold	gōld
hair	hāir

Level: Grade 5 #6

lot	lot
milk	milk
middle	mid′ dle
moment	mō′ ment
natural	nat′ ū răl
per	pẽr
possible	pos′ si ble
pounds	pounds
quiet	quī′ et
sail	sāil
scale	sc̦āle
someone	sŏme′ one

QUICKIE WORDS

Level: Grade 5 #7

speed	speed
tiny	tī ny
stone	stōne
Africa	Af′ ri ça
angle	añ′ gle
bear	beãr
beat	bēat
bottom.	bot′ tŏm
couldn't	coụld′ n't
died	dĩed
dress	dress
exactly	ex aç t′ ly

Level: Grade 5 #8

fight	fight (fīt)
fraction	fraç′ tion
fingers	fiñ′ gẽrs
French	French
hole	hōle
iron	ĩ′ ron (ĩ′ ũrn)
killed	killed
let's	let's
melody	mel′ ō dy
poor	poọr
remain	rē māin′
rolled	rōlled

Level: Grade 5 #9

smiled	smīled
trip	trip
surprise	sũr prĩṣe′
wonder	wŏn′ dẽr
burning	bũrn′ ing
catch	çatch (kach)
cents	cents
climbed	çlīmbed
design	dē sĩgn′
ears	ēars
else	else
England	Eñg′ land

Level: Grade 5 #10

foot	foot
grass	grȧss
gas	gas
grew	grew (grủ)
itself	it self′
joined	joined
key	kēy
law	lạw
least	lēast
plains	plāinṣ
row	rōw
shouted	shout′ ed

Level: Grade 5 #11

skin	skin
wrote	wrōte
valley	val′ ley
you're	yöu′re
alone	ȧ lōne′
bad	bad
brown	brown
cloud	çloud
cool	çoọl
decimal	dec′ i mǎl
drawing	drạw′ ing
east	ēast

Level: Grade 5 #12

engine	en′ gine
experiment	ex per′ i ment
equal	ē′ quǎl
express	ex press′
information	in foṛ mā′ tion
lost	lọst
mouth	mouth
pay	pāy
president	preṣ′ i dent
save	sāve
sent	sent
single	siñ′ gle

QUICKIE WORDS

Level: Grade 5 #13

symbols	sym′ bŏls
trouble	troub′ le (trub′ l)
touch	tŏuch
wear	weãr
yard	yärd
bank	bañk
bit	bit
choose	choọse
clean	cḻēan
coast	cọ̄ast
control	cọn trōl′
garden	gär′ den

Level: Grade 5 #14

party	pär′ ty
please	plēaṣe
period	pē′ ri ŏd
practice	praḏ′ tice
received	rē cēived′
report	rē pōrt′
rise	rīṣe
seeds	seeds
statement	stāte′ ment
stick	stick
straight	strāight (strāt)
strange	strär ḏe

Level: Grade 5 #15

strange	strānġe
visit	viṣ′ it
suppose	sup pōṣe′
whose	whöṣe
wire	wīre
woman	wom′ ăn (woom′)
yourself	yöur self′
art	ärt
break	breāk
business	buṣi′ ness
captain	ḏap′ tain (-tin)
caught	ḏauught

Level: Grade 5 #16

child	chīld
desert	dē ṣert′ or deṣ′ ẽrt
cost	cọ̄ost
direct	di reḏt′
feeling	feel′ ing
fell	fell
flow	flōw
God	God
history	his′ tō ry
human	hū′ măn
hunting	hunt′ ing
increase	in cḻease′

Level: Grade 5 #17

lady	lā′ dy
ring	ring
maybe	māy′ bē
separate	sep′ ȧ rāte
serve	sẽrve
students	stū′ dents
team	tēam
uncle	uñ′ cle
aunt	ȧunt
cousin	cŏuṣ′ in
grandmother	grand′ mŏth ẽr
nephew	neph′ ew

Spelling Pretest

Date: Name:

raised		
razed		
pray		
prey		
pore		
pour		
please		
pleas		
bell		
belle		
plumb		
plum		

Level: 4   Number: 1

Spelling Pretest

Date: Name:

board		
bored		
blue		
blew		
piece		
peace		
new		
knew		
gnu		
arc		
ark		

Level: 4   Number: 2

Spelling Pretest

Date: Name:

abrupt		
construct		
annul		
instruct		
intrust		
discuss		
deduct		
result		
across		
adopt		
belong		
agree		

Level: 4   Number: 3

Spelling Pretest

Date: Name:

asleep		
decree		
esteem		
degree		
attire		
entice		
entire		
incline		
incite		
invite		
oblige		
perspire		

Level: 4   Number: 4

Spelling Pretest

Date: Name:

contact		
hobby		
forest		
lofty		
nostril		
product		
problem		
torrent		
huddle		
public		
pungent		
publish		

Level: 4   Number: 5

Spelling Pretest

Date: Name:

cadence		
pavement		
native		
equal		
freedom		
meeting		
Friday		
migrate		
tribal		
crisis		
hydrant		
silent		

Level: 4   Number: 6

Spelling Pretest

Date: Name:

beard		
eaves		
crease		
heave		
leap		
knee		
spleen		
frank		
smack		
clamp		
build		
built		

Level: 4   Number: 7

Spelling Pretest

Date: Name:

walk		
lawn		
chalk		
fault		
spawn		
drift		
fund		
verse		
search		
fern		
serve		
were		

Level: 4   Number: 8

Spelling Pretest

Date: Name:

ennoble		
elopement		
exponent		
heroic		
detachment		
dogmatic		
dramatic		
ecstatic		
elastic		
inducement		
acumen		

Level: 4   Number: 9

Spelling Pretest

Date: Name:

accusing		
amusement		
allurement		
establish		
fanatic		
fantastic		
gigantic		
inhabit		
abusive		
perusal		
pursuant		
refusal		

Level: 4   Number: 10

Spelling Pretest

Date: Name:

sulfuric		
assemblage		
appendix		
attendant		
intestate		
compensate		
strait		
straight		
rote		
wrote		
wave		
waive		

Level: 4 Number: 11

Spelling Pretest

Date: Name:

boll		
bowl		
nose		
knows		
rein		
rain		
reign		
paws		
pause		
pride		
pried		

Level: 4   Number: 12

Spelling Pretest

afloat		
bemoan		
below		
bestow		
deplore		
postpone		
discourse		
deport		
remote		
dilute		
ensue		
demure		

Level: 4   Number: 13

Spelling Pretest

Date: Name:

abreast		
befriend		
ahead		
behead		
attempt		
distress		
amidst		
eclipse		
extinct		
forgive		
inflect		
inflict		

Level: 4   Number: 14

Spelling Pretest

Date: Name:

austere		
revere		
bequeath		
beseech		
decrease		
increase		
demean		
repeal		
appeal		
appear		
appease		
blaspheme		

Level: 4   Number: 15

Spelling Pretest

Date: Name:

discreet		
extreme		
entreat		
impeach		
awry		
beguile		
deprive		
describe		
despise		
prescribe		
decline		
requite		

Level: 4   Number: 16

90

Spelling Pretest

Date: Name:

domestic		
embezzle		
embellish		
parental		
poetic		
presented		
preventive		
refreshing		
replenish		
surrender		
redundant		
concurrent		

Level: 4   Number: 17

Spelling Pretest

Date: Name:

abolish		
accomplish		
abhorrent		
admonish		
allotment		
colossus		
demolish		
harmonic		
imposter		
laconic		
apostate		
embody		

Level: 4   Number: 18

Spelling Pretest

Date: Name:

hart		
heart		
hear		
here		
heard		
herd		
him		
hymn		
hole		
whole		
hour		
our		

Level: 4   Number: 19

Spelling Pretest

Date: Name:

in		
inn		
key		
quay		
rhyme		
rime		
knot		
not		
know		
no		
hi		
high		

Level: 4   Number: 20

Spelling Pretest

gladden		
ravel		
happen		
sadden		
freshen		
open		
lengthen		
quicken		
written		
glisten		
drunken		
mutton		

Level: 4   Number: 21

Spelling Pretest

Date: Name:

crayon		
omen		
siphon		
barrel		
parcel		
aspen		
cabin		
dragon		
gravel		
bevel		
sudden		
lemon		

Level: 4   Number: 22

Spelling Pretest

Date: Name:

credence		
fracas		
greedy		
gateway		
namesake		
measles		
people		
legion		
region		
steeple		
cipher		
highland		

Spelling Pretest

Date: Name:

arrow		
narrow		
harrow		
sparrow		
shallow		
shadow		
mellow		
meadow		
window		
widow		
borrow		
fallow		

Spelling Pretest

grieve		
retrieve		
thieve		
relief		
achieving		
relieve		
believe		
pieced		
conceit		
deceitful		
sheik		

Level: 4   Number: 25

Spelling Pretest

Date: Name:

bald		
bawled		
bear		
bare		
be		
bee		
air		
ere		
e'er		
heir		
aisle		
isle		

Spelling Pretest

Date: Name:

clever		
wayward		
painter		
digest		
lightning		
portrait		
novice		
climate		
scaffold		
transcript		
menace		
shepherd		

Level: 4   Number: 27

101

Spelling Pretest

Date: Name:

wholesome		
button		
jostle		
picnic		
grumble		
trouble		
sarcasm		
tarnish		
relapse		
profess		
revenge		
flighty		

Level: 4   Number: 28

Spelling Pretest

Date: Name:

educate		
effigy		
ebony		
elephant		
embassy		
exodus		
felony		
genesis		
federal		
penitent		
fellowship		
resident		

Level: 4   Number: 29

Spelling Pretest

Date: Name:

bail		
bale		
base		
bass		
beach		
beech		
beat		
beet		
bin		
been		
bold		
bowled		

Level: 4   Number: 30

Spelling Pretest

Date: Name:

berth		
birth		
cast		
caste		
cede		
seed		
coarse		
course		
cane		
Cain		
wry		
rye		

Level: 4   Number: 31

Spelling Pretest

Date: Name:

tonnage		
worry		
wonder		
novel		
booty		
movement		
stucco		
buzzard		
custard		
hundred		
husband		
buckle		

Level: 4

Spelling Pretest

Date: Name:

reptile		
sentence		
refuse		
speckle		
sterile		
Wednesday		
zealous		
dictate		
pillage		
tribute		
bramble		
callous		

Level: 4   Number: 33

Spelling Pretest

Date: Name:

cell		
sell		
cent		
sent		
scent		
chased		
chaste		
clause		
claws		
cord		
chord		

Level: 4

Number: 34

Spelling Pretest

Date: Name:

conceal		
absolve		
congeal		
dissolve		
respond		
begrudge		
convulse		
repulse		
indulge		
succumb		
affront		
among		

Level: 4   Number: 35

Spelling Pretest

Date: Name:

refrain		
restrain		
remain		
retain		
retail		
reprint		
restrict		
submit		
reproach		
patrol		
before		
retrace		

Spelling Pretest

Date: Name:

fashion		
knapsack		
galley		
ladder		
lattice		
passive		
practice		
rapid		
rabid		
tactics		
biscuit		
image		

Level: 4   Number: 37

Spelling Pretest

Date: Name:

alkali		
asterisk		
alkaline		
bachelor		
fabricate		
galaxy		
mariner		
paragraph		
paragon		
paraphrase		
cherubim		
density		

Level: 4   Number: 38

Spelling Pretest

Date: Name:

expedite		
petulant		
pediment		
pelican		
recompose		
spherical		
currency		
subterfuge		
nullify		
subsidy		
fiftieth		
miracle		

Level: 4   Number: 39

Spelling Pretest

Date: Name:

rigorous		
synonym		
nimbleness		
wilderness		
conjugate		
controvert		
consecrate		
coronet		
dominate		
arbitrate		
armament		

Spelling Pretest

Date: Name:

decimal		
emphasis		
despotism		
epitaph		
lethargy		
pentateuch		
metaphor		
editor		
senator		
seraphim		
specimen		
speculate		

Level: 4   Number: 41

Spelling Pretest

Date: Name:

criticism		
mystery		
cylinder		
mystify		
physical		
typify		
judgement		
common		
dogma		
dolphin		
hostile		
modern		

Level: 4   Number: 42

Spelling Pretest

Date: Name:

gage		
gauge		
gate		
gait		
gilt		
guilt		
great		
grate		
grease		
Greece		
groan		
grown		

Spelling Pretest

alert		
avert		
assert		
concern		
pervert		
expert		
inert		
infer		
insert		
invert		
prefer		
subvert		

Spelling Pretest

Date: Name:

superb		
recur		
absurd		
demur		
disturb		
remove		
aloof		
balloon		
buffoon		
avail		
await		
decay		

Level: 4   Number: 45

Spelling Pretest

Date: Name:

prevail		
abstain		
reclaim		
acquaint		
assuage		
blockade		
display		
entail		
obtain		
contain		
persuade		
recall		

Spelling Pretest

Date: Name:

alpha		
damask		
bracket		
padlock		
placid		
Sabbath		
stagnant		
mandate		
stagnate		
comfort		
other		
mother		

Level: 4   Number: 47

Spelling Pretest

Date: Name:

legate		
message		
membrane		
rescue		
flout		
meant		
quick		
solve		
wrong		
shrimp		
cause		
gauze		

Spelling Pretest

Date: Name:

squaw		
afraid		
cross		
contempt		
command		
commence		
commend		
complaint		
approach		
curtail		
repute		
skirmish		

Spelling Pretest

Date: Name:

fervency		
nursery		
mercury		
perjury		
artery		
harmony		
harmonize		
affluent		
barrier		
barrister		
carrion		
baluster		

Spelling Pretest

Date: Name:

flagrancy		
radiance		
fragrance		
slavery		
maintenance		
dialect		
diagram		
diary		
ivory		
pliable		
pedestal		
medicine		

Level: 4   Number: 51

125

Spelling Pretest

Date: Name:

field		
fiend		
thief		
shriek		
yield		
fierce		
pierce		
niece		
crock		
shock		
mock		
league		

Spelling Pretest

Date: Name:

false		
swarm		
quart		
thwart		
sought		
bought		
bright		
plight		
pitch		
stitch		
hitch		
patch		

Level: 4   Number: 53

Spelling Pretest

Date: Name:

batch		
latch		
match		
edge		
hedge		
ledge		
wedge		
bridge		
ridge		
hinge		
cringe		
bilge		

Level: 4   Number: 54

Spelling Pretest

Date: Name:

hall		
haul		
hay		
hey		
hare		
hair		
heal		
heel		
hire		
higher		
hoop		
whoop		

Level: 4   Number: 55

Spelling Pretest

Date: Name:

faith		
strange		
scrape		
greet		
perch		
champ		
drench		
squeeze		
grist		
shrink		
theme		

Spelling Pretest

Date: Name:

chime		
badge		
smart		
dodge		
brawl		
dwarf		
grant		
spunk		
length		
launch		
pledge		
screech		

Level: 4   Number: 57

Spelling Pretest

Date: Name:

knight		
night		
knave		
nave		
loan		
lone		
links		
lynx		
loch		
lock		
lax		
lacks		

Level: 4   Number: 58

Spelling Pretest

Date: Name:

alien		
union		
savior		
senior		
junior		
spaniel		
valiant		
indian		
onion		
brilliant		
million		
trillion		

Level: 4   Number: 59

Spelling Pretest

Date: Name:

anger		
anguish		
angry		
dangle		
jingle		
mangle		
wrangle		
longer		
stronger		
bungle		
hunger		
languish		

Spelling Pretest

Date:

Name:

surely		
sugar		
sureness		
censure		
pressure		
issue		
tissue		
assure		
insure		
assurance		
insurance		
insurer		

Level: 4

Number: 61

Spelling Pretest

Date: Name:

condense		
dispense		
defense		
expense		
incense		
immense		
offense		
pretense		
suspense		
license		
intense		
nonsense		

Level: 4   Number: 62

Spelling Pretest

amalgamate		
facilitate		
assassinate		
coagulate		
concatenate		
confabulate		
congratulate		
contaminate		
decapitate		
circus		
elaborate		
cheese		

Level: 4   Number: 63

Spelling Pretest

Date: Name:

furnace		
nervous		
furlong		
purchase		
surface		
capacity		
comparison		
comparative		
compatible		
declarative		
diagonal		
diameter		

Level: 4   Number: 64

138

Spelling Pretest

Date: Name:

dogmatically		
depravity		
ambassador		
ambient		
calamine		
juvenile		
pedigree		
register		
revelry		
skeptical		
verily		
halcyon		

Level: 4   Number: 65

Spelling Pretest

Date: Name:

brassiere		
graze		
glazier		
seizure		
hosiery		
fusion		
azure		
measure		
pleasure		
evasion		
invasion		
persuasion		

Congratulations!

Your child has successfully completed Level 4 of

Success in Spelling.

You may use any remaining school weeks to learn the Quickie Words in the following pages. Use the same teaching methods as you have used during the study of Success in Spelling.

Your child is now ready to move on to Level 5.

Spelling Pretest

Date: Name:

appear		
buy		
baby		
care		
century		
cross		
either		
everything		
factors		
floor		
hill		
ice		

Level: Grade 5   Number: 1

Spelling Pretest

Date: Name:

jumped		
outside		
metal		
pushed		
result		
ride		
sleep		
snow		
solve		
son		
speak		
tall		

Level: Grade 5   Number: 2

Spelling Pretest

Date: Name:

village		
bed		
already		
bright		
consonant		
copy		
dictionary		
ease		
everyone		
free		
hope		
instead		

Spelling Pretest

Date: Name:

lake		
lead		
laughed		
method		
nation		
phrase		
section		
quite		
soil		
spring		
temperature		
themselves		

Level: Grade 5   Number: 4

Spelling Pretest

Date: Name:

type		
act		
within		
age		
although		
amount		
broken		
build		
count		
eat		
gold		
hair		

Level: Grade 5   Number: 5

Spelling Pretest

lot		
milk		
middle		
moment		
natural		
per		
possible		
pounds		
quiet		
sail		
scale		
someone		

Level: Grade 5   Number: 6

Spelling Pretest

Date: Name:

speed		
tiny		
stone		
Africa		
angle		
bear		
beat		
bottom		
couldn't		
died		
dress		
exactly		

Level: Grade 5   Number: 7

Spelling Pretest

Date: Name:

fight		
fraction		
fingers		
French		
hole		
iron		
killed		
let's		
melody		
poor		
remain		
rolled		

Level: Grade 5   Number: 8

Spelling Pretest

Date: Name:

smiled		
trip		
surprise		
wonder		
burning		
catch		
cents		
climbed		
design		
ears		
else		
England		

Level: Grade 5   Number: 9

150

Spelling Pretest

Date: Name:

foot		
grass		
gas		
grew		
itself		
joined		
key		
law		
least		
plains		
row		
shouted		

Level: Grade 5   Number: 10

Spelling Pretest

Date: Name:

skin		
wrote		
valley		
you're		
alone		
bad		
brown		
cloud		
cool		
decimal		
drawing		
east		

Level: Grade 5   Number: 11

Spelling Pretest

Date: Name:

engine		
experiment		
equal		
express		
information		
lost		
mouth		
pay		
president		
save		
sent		
single		

Level: Grade 5   Number: 12

153

Spelling Pretest

Date: Name:

symbols		
trouble		
touch		
wear		
yard		
bank		
bit		
choose		
clean		
coast		
control		
garden		

Level: Grade 5   Number: 13

Spelling Pretest

Date: Name:

party		
please		
period		
practice		
received		
report		
rise		
seeds		
statement		
stick		
straight		
strange		

Level: Grade 5   Number: 14

Spelling Pretest

Date: Name:

strange		
visit		
suppose		
whose		
wire		
woman		
yourself		
art		
break		
business		
captain		
caught		

Level: Grade 5   Number: 15

Spelling Pretest

Date: Name:

child		
desert		
cost		
direct		
feeling		
fell		
flow		
God		
history		
human		
hunting		
increase		

Level: Grade 5   Number: 16

Spelling Pretest

Date: Name:

lady		
ring		
maybe		
separate		
serve		
students		
team		
uncle		
aunt		
cousin		
grandmother		
nephew		

Level: Grade 5   Number: 17

Spelling Pretest

Date: Name:

Level: Number: